Comparing Past and Present

Cooking and Eating

Rebecca Rissman

Heinemann
LIBRARY

Chicago, Illinois

To contact Capstone Global Library please phone 800-747-4992, or visit our website www.capstonepub.com

Edited by Rebecca Rissman, Daniel Nunn, and
  Catherine Veitch
Designed by Philippa Jenkins
Picture research by Elizabeth Alexander
Production by Helen McCreath
Originated by Capstone Global Library Ltd
Printed in the United States of America in
North Mankato, MN. 082014 008425RP

Library of Congress Cataloging-in-Publication Data
Rissman, Rebecca.
  Cooking and eating / Rebecca Rissman.
    pages cm.—(Comparing past and present)
  Includes bibliographical references and index.
  ISBN 978-1-4329-8990-3 (hardback)—ISBN 978-1-4329-9024-4 (paperback) 1. Cooking—Juvenile literature. 2. Cooking—History—Juvenile literature. 3. Food habits—Juvenile literature. I. Title.
  TX652.5.R59 2014
  641.5—dc23   2013012539

Acknowledgments
We would like to thank the following for permission to reproduce photographs: Alamy pp. 4 (© Wolverhampton City Council - Arts and Heritage), 7 (© Blend Images), 12 (© Elizabeth Whiting & Associates); Corbis pp. 8 (A. W. Cutler/National Geographic Society), 20 (© Minnesota Historical Society); Getty Images pp. 10 (Hulton Archive), 14 (Chicago History Museum), 16 (Haywood Magee/Picture Post/Hulton Archive), 18 (Gerry Crannam/Fox Photos), 23 (Hulton Archive); Shutterstock pp. 5 (© wavebreakmedia), 9 (© Gr8), 11 (© Tatjana Kruusma), 13 (© Yeko Photo Studio), 15 (© kazoka), 19 (© Monkey Business Images), 21 (© Kzenon), 23 (© Tatjana Kruusma), 23 (© kazoka); Superstock pp. 6, 17 (age footstock), 22.

Front cover photographs of two girls making doughnuts, 1925, reproduced with permission of Corbis (© Bettmann), and a woman using an electric mixer reproduced with permission of Getty Images (Nacivet/Photographer's Choice). Back cover photograph of a woman and children cooking reproduced with permission of Superstock.

We would like to thank Nancy Harris and Diana Bentley for their invaluable help in the preparation of this book.

Every effort has been made to contact copyright holders of material reproduced in this book. Any omissions will be rectified in subsequent printings if notice is given to the publisher.

Contents

Comparing the Past and Present

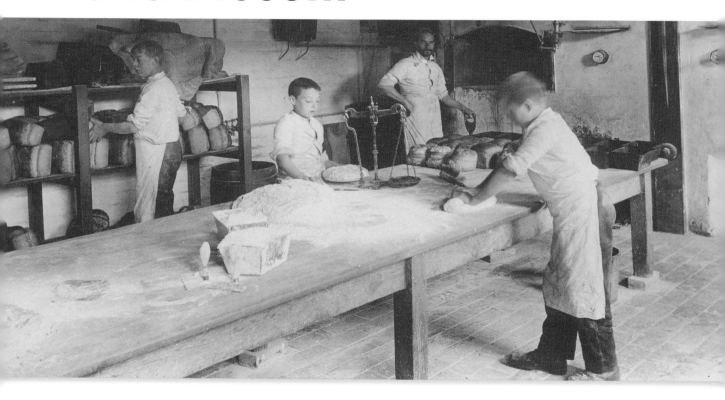

Things in the past have already happened.

Things in the present are
happening now.

Cooking has changed over time.

The way people cook today
is very different from the past.

Kitchens

In the past, some kitchens were outdoors.

Today, most kitchens are indoors.

Kitchen Appliances

In the past, ovens were heated by burning wood.

Today, some ovens are heated
by electricity.

In the past, people did not have refrigerators. They kept food for a short time.

Today, people have refrigerators.
They can keep food for a
longer time.

water pump

In the past, some people did not have running water. They pumped water from under the ground.

Today, people get running water
from the faucet.

Cooking

In the past, cooking meals took a long time.

Today, people can cook a meal
in a short time.

Getting Food

In the past, some people grew vegetables to eat. Some people also kept animals to eat.

Today, people buy most of their food at the store.

Eating Food

In the past, people ate food that was grown where they lived.

Today, people eat food from
around the world.

Then and Now

In the past, many children helped cook meals. Today, many children still help cook meals.

Picture Glossary

 **electricity** power that makes machines work

 **oven** kitchen tool used to cook food

 **running water** water that flows from a faucet

Index

Note to Parents and Teachers

Before reading

Talk to children about the difference between the past and present. Explain that the conversation you are having with them is taking place in the present. Then ask children to remember what they did last week. Explain that those activities took place in the past.

After reading

- Explain to children that the way people cook has changed over time. Ask children to name one or two of their favorite foods. Then, as a group, brainstorm about how the preparation method may have changed over time (e.g. in the past, people would not have purchased cake mix from the store; in the past, people might have raised their own chickens for eggs, etc.).

- Ask children to make a list of common kitchen equipment, such as microwave ovens, refrigerators, and mixers. Once children have finished their lists, ask them to cross off every item that would not have existed 100 years ago. Discuss their answers with the group.

- Have children turn to pages 16—17. Ask them to make a list of differences between the images. Record their observations on the board. As a group, discuss how cooking has changed over time.